Frontispiece. Contemporary. *In a framed plaque against a brick wall, a skilled interpreter of Japanese styles arranges honeysuckle (interrupting the frame with one piece of the vine) and white azaleas in vases set into openings in a pair of bamboo hangers the two arrangements nicely balanced in an enclosed but uncrowded space. Arranged by Lee Early Quinn.*

FLOWERS, SPACE, AND MOTION

New Designs
in Hanging Flower Arrangements

by Helen Van Pelt Wilson

SIMON AND SCHUSTER
NEW YORK

SBN 671-20965-5
Library of Congress Catalog Card Number: 71-159141
Designed by Jeanne Smith Pollack
Manufactured in the United States of America
By Kingsport Press, Kingsport, Tenn.

For Lois Wilson
Dear Friend and Valued Adviser

With Many Thanks

To Marianna Brockway of Westport, Connecticut, master judge, floral designer with both taste and technique, for her devoted interest and advice, her considerable contribution to the illustrations—her party decorations, her modern designs incorporating space and motion, and her environmental studies—and to George Taloumis and G. C. Bradbury, her photographers.

To Lee Early Quinn of Williamsburg, Virginia, trained in Japan, for the skillful and sensitive interpretations of Ikebana—traditional and free-form—that she designed and had photographed for this book.

To Frances Bode of Sacramento, California, for designs illustrating sculptural and other trends, and to W. T. Bode, the photographer of her work.

To Marguerite Bozarth of Seattle, Washington, for the fine hanging arrangements made for this book, and also for the many illustrations provided through the years for my calendar and magazine articles, and to C. Fanders, her photographer.

To all the other skilled designers whose interpretations here illustrate the trends of our times.

Finally, I am particularly grateful to Dorothy Riester—sculptor, lecturer, and writer—for her careful analysis of this text and professional assessment of the illustrations, and also for education in the principles of design that she has given me through the years.

Helen Van Pelt Wilson

Westport, Connecticut
January, 1971

Contents

Flower Arrangers Represented

MRS. R. E. AGNEW

FRANCES BODE

LILLIAN L. BODINE

MARGUERITE BOZARTH

NELDA H. BRANDENBURGER

MARIANNA BROCKWAY

MRS. DOUGLAS P. BRYCE

MRS. WILLIAM BURGER

STELLA COE

MRS. MERRITT ENGLAND

MARLIE L. ERWIN

MRS. ROSWELL E. FISHER

MRS. FRED J. HAY

HARRIET KENNEY

MRS. CHRISTOPHER Z. KING

BERNICE KINNEY

MARY G. KNIGHT

HARRY A. LAZIER

MRS. JAMES E. MCGRAW

BARBARA S. MEISSE

MURIEL L. MERRELL

MRS. WALTER E. MORRIS

ETSUKO MURAI

LEE EARLY QUINN

LUCY SARGENT

LAWRENCE TAYLOR

KASUMI TESHIGAHARA

MARY E. THOMPSON

LOIS WILSON

Artists Represented

ALEXANDER ARCHIPENKO: *Dance,* 1912

ROBERT BART: *Untitled,* 1964

SANDRO BOTTICELLI: *Birth of Venus*

DAVID BURT: *Emergence,* 1969
        Orbital Dance, 1968
        Pisces, 1968

ALEXANDER CALDER: *Snow Flurry,* 1948
        Spider, 1939

MARY CALLERY: *Composition 19—Symbol A,* 1960

JOSÉ DE RIVERA: *Construction 8,* 1954

NAUM GABO: *Column,* 1923

STEPHEN GILBERT: *Structure 14c,* 1961

BARBARA HEPWORTH: *Curved Form with Inner Form (Anima),* 1959

NANKOKU HIDAI: *Work 63-14-3,* 1963

IBRAM LASSAW: *Nebula in Orion,* 1951

SEYMOUR LIPTON: *Imprisoned Figure,* 1948

HENRY MOORE: *The Bride,* 1939–1940
        Reclining Figure, 1938

ANTOINE PEVSNER: *Twinned Column,* 1947

PABLO PICASSO: *Construction in Wire,* 1928–1929

UNKNOWN: *Figure of Man Leaning on Staff,* 900–1200 A.D.

9

Flowers, Space, and Motion

Space and Motion in the Arts
—Introduction

Art formerly reproductive has become creative.
—*Naum Gabo*

1. Hanging Decoration. *Suspended at eye level or above, charm-ing arrangements like this are set off by the larger space around them and made interesting by smaller spaces within the designs. Here, a rounded split-bamboo basket suggests the selection of circular elements—round creamy-lavender chrysanthemums and rounded leaf clusters of dark green ternstroemia. Asymmetry results from the balancing of the visually heavy basket with flowers and the force of the two short upright foliages against the long down-sweeping branch that utilizes space as a positive element. Arranged by Marguerite Bozarth.*

Like the ancient Roman god of doorways, the art of flower arrangement now faces in two directions. The private face is toward the home, its purpose to decorate, but in new ways; the public face is toward the exhibition hall or showroom, its purpose to design in the contemporary styles of the other arts, notably sculpture. In both situations, space around and within a design is seriously considered; in some cases, motion is also a factor.

Today, designers are more than ever concerned with the kinetics of composition, even with the motion or energy that is overt—as in whole arrangements electrically motivated, or with moving parts as in stamobiles—and never were floral designers more creative or more aware of the trends in other arts. The designs in Part III of this book are evidence of their interest and the attention they are paying to works seen in museums and art exhibitions. However, trends from the general artistic atmosphere also seem to reach designers since they tell me they have never seen the pieces their own work often resembles. Sculpture, in particular, stimulates the floral designer to a new plane of creativity.

The artist has long been aware of the value of space within and around his painting or sculpture. Consider Botticelli's *Birth of Venus*, painted in the fifteenth century. The three elements stand clear—the winds, the goddess, and the nymph. Motion is more than implicit. Here indeed design elements of space and motion are fully realized (photo 2).

As for sculpture, although pre-Columbian sculpture is full of openings, in the West the mass of stone was rarely penetrated until after Rodin. Then, and increasingly in the twentieth century, first Alexander Archipenko and Jacques Lipchitz, then Barbara Hepworth, and Henry Moore pierced the blocks so that the eye could move through and around their compositions, and space was no longer

2. Birth of Venus *by Sandro Botticelli. This painting illustrates a fifteenth-century artist's brilliant use of space and motion. Three elements stand clear. On the left, the winds rush in but do not touch the goddess, who stands apart in a spatial area of her own. On the right, the nymph approaches; she does not touch. The whirl of motion here is vivid, not implicit. Figures of the wind; locks of Venus, a delicate transition to the cloak; the nymph scarcely able to hold it—all attest to the sweep of the breeze. Space and motion are fully realized. The composition is contained in a frame, not only outside the picture but within by the horizon line across the back and the vertical trees on the right. To achieve stability, sculptors Lipton and others employ the same device today. The Uffizi Gallery, Florence, Italy.*

16

something to be filled (photos 3 to 6). Some sculptors stretched wire across openings to delay and emphasize the look-through aspect and to create still other volumes of space. Today there are sculptural forms with physical motion as well. In Alexander Calder's mobiles, designs change even as we look at them; some pieces move electrically and are illuminated by flashing lights.

In a recent visit to the Tate Gallery in London, I saw a four-foot mobile—I suppose the piece could be called that—made of four brilliantly painted strips suspended above an electric turntable, the whole enclosed in a glass case. The effect of motion and changing colors was so striking that visitors hardly looked at anything else in the area.

In the same gallery I saw a large framed design composed of horizontal wires, all in purple tones. The wires vibrated, and the shading changed as currents of air affected them. It was an interesting exhibit.

Then, attending a conference in Milwaukee, I took time off to visit the art museum there and found myself in a room entirely devoted to wall pieces (paintings?) that vibrated with changing colors and moving parts. I did not find this a restful experience, and I hope that flower arrangers who draw inspiration from contemporary art will not be carried away by this kind of thing. There was, of course, no plant material in any of these designs, and surely flower arrangement, even defined in the broadest terms, should include *some*, and this would seem obligatory in a standard show.

In the 1940s flower arrangers exposed to Oriental art after World War II became aware of space as a vital element in design. Turning from the colorful packed compositions of Flemish flower painting, which was their original inspiration, they began talking of voids in floral compositions, of occupied space versus empty space, of irregular outlines that brought outer areas into the design. Compare an eighteenth-century Williamsburg composition, tight with flowers and

3. Figure of Man Leaning on Staff, *900–1200* A.D. *This Huastec sculpture from northern Veracruz, an example of Indian work done in Mexico, illustrates a centuries-old artistic use of space. Such pre-Columbian finds strongly influenced twentieth-century sculptors, particularly Archipenko, Hepworth, and Moore, and now the flower arrangers who also employ space as a vital design element. Courtesy, The Museum of Primitive Art, New York.*

17

foliages and of regular outline, with a mid-twentieth-century mass arrangement. In the latter, open areas visible within flow into the space without. Interrupted contours define spatial areas adjacent to an arrangement, making these part of the composition as a whole.

Today, interest in space as something positive has been greatly emphasized since man has entered the vast space that surrounds the earth and has set his foot upon the moon. It is but natural that men, women, and children everywhere, small boys as well as artists, should be sensitive to such interests. The flower arranger, responsive to the world and to art as it is affected by prevailing taste and interest, is now more than ever seeing and utilizing space in exciting new ways. Motion also fascinates the designer. Line compositions imply motion; mobiles and stamobiles employ motion; stabiles suggest motion. And what is more natural than this preoccupation, since today we are rarely still but always in a whirlwind of motion.

Some sculptors seem to have fallen in love with motion *per se.* In fact, Filippo Tommaso Marinetti, leader of the Futurist Movement, made this remarkable statement as early as 1909: "The world's splendour has been enriched by a new beauty: the beauty of speed. . . . A racing motor-car, its frame adorned with great pipes, like snakes with explosive breath . . . a roaring motor-car, which looks as though running on shrapnel, is more beautiful than the *Victory of Samothrace.*"

About the word *new* in my subtitle, most of the illustrations in this book are brand new, that is, not published before, and many of them have been designed and photographed just for this book. The few that have been published before, I consider "new" in that they will always be in style like a dress from a good designer. In the twenty years in which I edited *The Flower Arrangement Calendar,* I saw many designs too excellent to disappear. In view of the present-day passion for change, however, I have included only a few of my favorites from the past.

I hope this book will set minds in motion too, so that flower arrangers will become even more creative through this late twentieth century in which we live and make our own rapid motions in space.

4. Dance, *1912*, ALEXANDER ARCHIPENKO. *An irregular oval of space dominates this rhythmic design of dancing figures. The sculptor, who invented a kind of three-dimensional Cubism and maintained that the object served as an excuse for the representation of motion in space, was involved with the void from the start of his work. Here is seen a handsome example of what we now term negative form. Courtesy, Perls Galleries, New York.*

5. Curved Form with Inner Form (Anima), *1959*, BARBARA HEP-
WORTH. *Opened to penetrate reality, this organic form employs
negative space within as a design element. Rounded rather than
angular, refined to an ultimate movement and intimate shape,
evolving and revolving, this example of her work is utterly simple
and subjective, a poetic statement. Collection of Everson Museum of Art, Syracuse, New York.*

6. The Bride, *1939–1940*, HENRY MOORE. *The look-through technique of copper wires, here stretched across cast lead, achieves
depth in an interesting way in sculpture, and can also do so in
floral designs that stand free (photo 23) or are suspended against
a wall. Here depth is experienced in three ways: through the long
outer wires, through the two sets of inner secondary wires, and
in the four concave areas of the sculpture itself. Sculptors have
long used the technique of concave-convex areas to delineate a
form, but here wires have trapped the space, which becomes as
important as the object itself. Collection, The Museum of Modern
Art, New York. Acquired through the Lillie P. Bliss Bequest.*

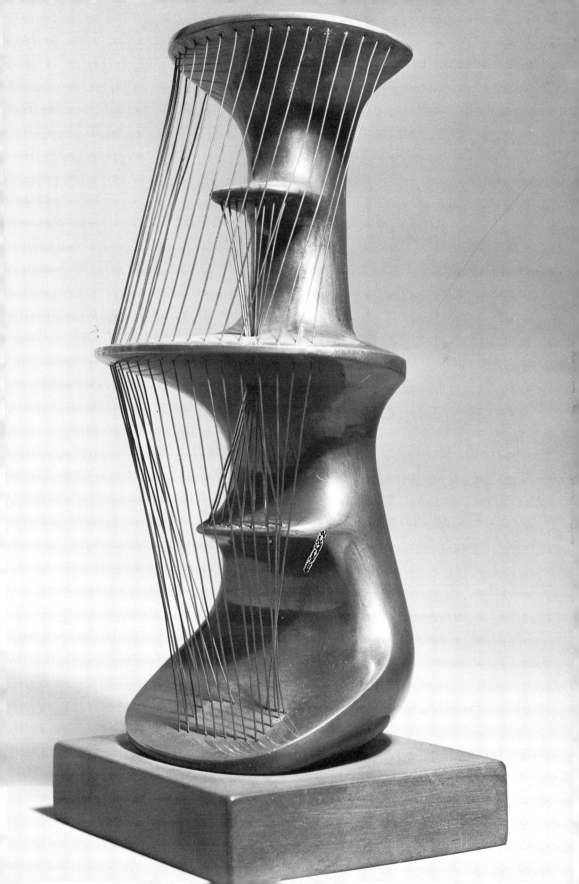

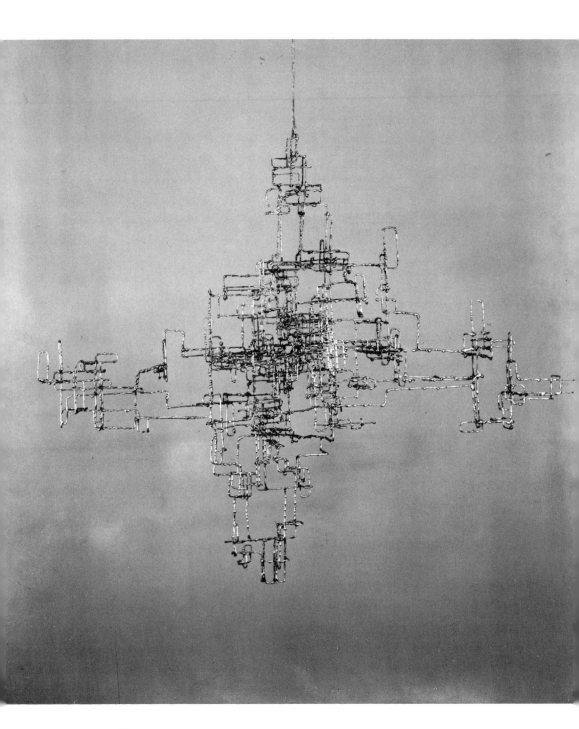

I

They Decorate Without Crowding
–for the Home

> *Not chaos-like together crushed and bruis'd,*
> *But, as the world, harmoniously confused:*
> *Where order in variety we see,*
> *And where, tho' all things differ, all agree.*
> —Alexander Pope

7. Nebula in Orion, *1951*, IBRAM LASSAW. *A welded hanging sculpture of bronze rods is reminiscent of many abstract shapes in nature and could be interpreted with straw, bamboo, or other thin-line material. This departs from the practice of treating all sculpture as an immovable object to be placed on a pedestal and reflects the mid-twentieth-century trend of lifting sculpture into space. Collection, The Museum of Modern Art, New York. Gift of Mrs. John D. Rockefeller 3rd.*

23

Today, home decorations are likely to be new in placement and far from traditional in design; they tend to be more informal and more colorful than exhibition pieces. Effects can be quite simple or rather complex and sophisticated, some of them suggesting Japanese work. In these, art sensitively reflects nature.

In Part I, arrangements are suspended in a space for which the eye defines the extent or frame; they also become part of a larger environment, the room. Hung in a bay window, dropped from a ceiling fixture, or responding to the air in a breezeway, these decorations at eye level or just above are practical, offering an amusing way with flowers that requires us to look up, not down, on their beauty. These arrangements are ideal for apartments or small living rooms, or, for that matter, large ones when there are many guests. Requiring no table area, high-up compositions, above the head of the tallest guest, avoid clutter while contributing to the gaiety of entertaining.

Arrangements in space are also practical for public rooms. They can be appreciated even when there is a crowd because they can be seen, as low table arrangements cannot. For really restricted areas, such as a church vestibule or a small foyer, they are a boon.

This concept of flowers in space is made even more attractive by the containers available today for high-up decorations. Some are planned for flowers, like the new and old Japanese baskets; some are "found" objects like birdcages. Each sets off its bright cargo when well selected to do so. And almost any container can be adapted for hanging with inconspicuous monofilament or by attaching a rope, a chain (brass dog chains are fine), lengths of velvet, silk cord, ribbon, or raffia loops; such suspensions will then become an element in the design. Ceramists produce one-of-a-kind pieces, and unusual containers of metal and wood can be found. Methods of attachment vary with ingenuity: picture hooks, iron hooks, ceiling hooks, birdcage

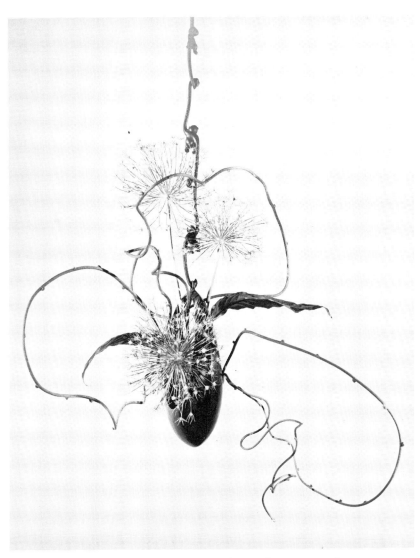

8. Suspended in Space. *A traditional Japanese bronze moon supports a contemporary design of triple spaces, with the open areas delineated by curves of actinidea, the triple idea accented by starbursts of 'Star of Persia' alliums. Spathiphyllum leaves, pointing out and down, emphasize the airy width of the decoration, its weight well supported by a heavy monkey chain. Arranged by Frances Bode.*

25

hangers—all give security if heavy enough, and also enough "play" for arrangements not to appear static.

In Japan, a hanging arrangement is designed in *kakebana* style. It is often placed in a tokonoma, or alcove, with a scroll on the wall and a tray sand-painting or another flower arrangement below on a table. The moon vase is a favorite, also a boat shape or basket. One flower may be featured, its beauty set off by a few leaves, a branch of evergreen, or a trailing vine. In several of the arrangements shown here, we see the subtle influence of the classical *kakebana* style, but freely interpreted, perhaps with a *nageire* grouping of flowers.

Most of the designs are purely Western, but all are floating, suspended rather than simply hanging. If an arrangement in the air "hangs heavy," it loses charm and defeats its decorative purpose. These designs are light and lifted; they successfully defy gravity.

WALL DECORATIONS

For the garden-minded, decorations of natural materials—collages or wall designs in open frames—fastened against a wall can be enjoyed as pictures. Semipermanent, if composed of driftwood and dried things, they are hung in winter and stored in summer, giving variety to decorations. We rarely move a fine oil painting about, yet we almost cease to see it so familiar does it become. On view for only part of the year, both pictures and well-designed natural decorations give pleasure as we rediscover them anew through fresh seasonal placements.

The collage is a design technique of pasting or otherwise attaching materials not always associated with one another, such as scraps of cloth, paper, bits of tin perhaps, to a particular background. In the arranger's hands, the collage is more often than not made of materials

9. Traditional. African-violets with a balancing fountain of grass hang over the edge of a traditional Japanese half-moon ceramic in a tokonoma, all this seen in counterpoint to a wall scroll, the verse by the arranger. A striking relationship exists between the two-dimensional use of line and space in the calligraphy by Taiku Tokuno and the three-dimensional line and space of the arrangement. Arranged by Etsuko Murai, Tokyo.

の衣中にて
花は散りける

associated in nature. Collages of dried flowers and foliages sometimes resemble old botanical prints with root, leaf, flower, bud, and seed of one subject carefully mounted.

Actually the collage is a twentieth-century technique in which each of the materials has its own validity and creates its own space. When the materials are flat, as pressed leaves, the space is illusionary, and the collage relates to the two-dimensional space of many contemporary paintings. When the materials are three-dimensional, as seeds, cones, branches, and most natural forms, the collage relates to sculpture and the shallow real space of bas-relief.

10. From the Mountains. *Five pale pink native rhododendrons with their own handsome dark leaves are grouped in an adequately heavy brown Mexican basket suspended by a linked monkey chain. A can of water in the basket keeps the flowers fresh, the woody ends of the branches split to insure absorption. Arranged by Marguerite Bozarth.*

FOR PARTIES

One snowy Easter day I was grateful that all the decorations were "hung" instead of "set." An egg hunt in my fern garden is traditional for the family children. When snow made it impossible, treasures were hidden about the house while interested parents—a great many of them—stood about to watch. Happily, there were no elbow-height arrangements to be knocked over. Even dining-table space was conserved. My friend Marianna Brockway hung lovely flower pieces all over the house: on the front door, a modern May basket; from the dining-room chandelier, a marvelous Easter-egg and daisy concoction; in my bedroom a lacy affair silhouetted in space against the light, with a smaller version in my bathroom. Also enjoyed by young and old— we ranged from five to eighty-three years—was a mobile of blown-and-decorated eggs suspended from a bare branch. This present from the Peter Kenney family (Harriet designed it as well as others in this book) was hung at an east window above a radiator, whose gentle heat waves kept the mobile in entrancing motion.

For a summer wedding here, floral pieces were hung on the lamp-post and front door, and beribboned roses were suspended from the chandelier to leave the wedding cake in full glory on the table. When a caterer's tent covers the buffet area, great half spheres of flowers can be locked at the apex of the supporting poles. This is a delightful new type of high-up decoration.

For Thanksgiving, when the board is groaning, to say the least, it is convenient and a change too to put the fruit decoration above the table instead of on it and to hang a swag beside the mantel.

For Christmas, decorations in the air are a delight—the chandelier in the dining room trimmed like a Christmas tree, poinsettias in beautiful suspension in the hall, perhaps a glass ring for an apartment door.

(Photos 30 through 47 show these party decorations.)

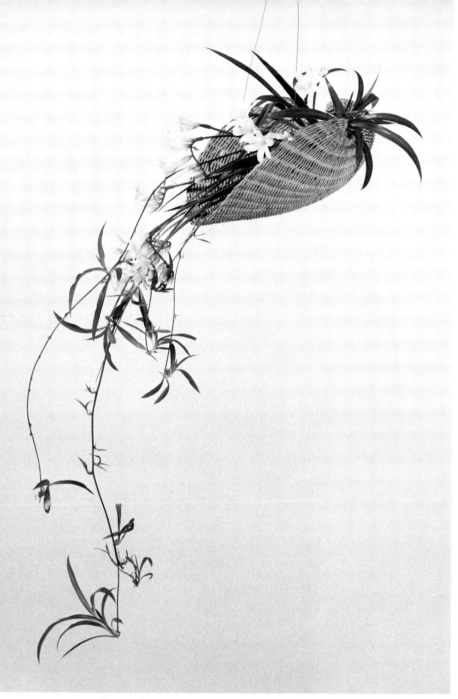

11. Cascade. A shell-shaped basket, suspended on wires, brings late-winter beauty and fragrance indoors. A heavy pinholder set in a jar of water at the closed end supports the trailing stems of spider plant and the clusters of white freesias that spill from the basket. Arranged by Mrs. Fred J. Hay.

30

12. From the Sea. *Black kelp from the California coast and two brilliant cerise crape-myrtle blossoms are combined in a linear design reminiscent of Mary Callery's* Symbol A *(photo 84). Suspended on a brass chain, the flowers kept fresh in a hidden container of water, this design has a living quality, forceful rather than simply pretty. Arranged by Bernice Kinney.*

13. Country Piece. *An early fall arrangement suspended in the doorway of a patio moves with the breeze. In the unglazed cream-colored jar splashed with yellow glaze, dark fern fronds and golden yarrow, both country materials, associate well and are suited to the nageire style, which is naive and unaffected so as to reveal the beauty of the flowers in a natural manner. The central weight of the asymmetric design and the short flower-and-fern spray on the right balance the thrust into space of the longer material on the left, and the rope triangle contributes to the design. (Native ferns stay fresh after conditioning for an hour or so in deep water. If fronds are going to wilt, they do so at once, so those that stay fresh in water remain so in an arrangement.) Arranged by Marguerite Bozarth.*

Boat Designs. *14. Above. A smooth Japanese bamboo boat, suspended by a brass chain, holds a spray of deep rose camellias in a frame of their own shining leaves, and a branch of purple plum, the horizontal of the boat nicely repeated by the plant material. 15. Below. A boat design of rough weathered wood, suspended on wires, holds a double design of scarlet tulips and red flowering quince on the left, balanced by a quince branch openly pruned and placed to fall below the line of the wood on the right. Arranged by Lee Early Quinn.*

32

16. Camellias. *A candleholder, gray-blue over brown, is suspended by hemp ropes, the round perforations of the metal associating with the shape of the flowers. The curve of the budded branch of pink 'Debutante' camellias and dark glossy leaves moves gracefully from a high-up bud tip to a low accent flower. Variety in the shape of the spaces adds interest to this uncluttered design. Arranged by Mrs. Fred J. Hay.*

17. Orange and Purple. *A collage-abstract is developed with ceramic containers, made by the arranger, supporting stylized and geometric plant materials—a tight vertical bundle of dark green equisetum, a sheared mass of purple statice, and three golden daylilies. This abstract is placed to the side of a collage made from layers of paper with scatterings of chipped glass between and from glass-threaded plastic fabric in orange and purple hues affixed to a yellow background. The two-dimensional background and three-dimensional foreground, with the interrelated color harmony, employ spatial concepts in a highly sophisticated way. Arranged by Mrs. Walter E. Morris.*

18. Radiation. *In this controlled design, two 'Sterling Silver' roses emerge from a bronze fish container. The euonymus vine on the left associates with a right hand spray to inscribe a wide space, the hooked ends of both drawing the eye back to the center. Two iris leaves serve a special purpose: The one on the right helps control balance; the one on the left marks off another interesting space with the left-hand vine. The roses are set off in a space of their own, the straight stem of the one paralleling the line of the chain. Somehow the angled leaf and the fish container have a whimsical effect. Arranged by Marguerite Bozarth.*

19. Asymmetric Suspension. *Brown Japanese ceramics hold well-related arrangements of lemon-yellow yarrow, variegated iris leaves, and bunching onions, with interest increased by the two-level suspension. The solid rounded container is nicely related to the round opening of the pear-shaped one with an onion stem moving across as transition and closing a long oval central space above. The outward thrusts of iris leaves contribute to the asymmetric balance. Arranged by Frances Bode.*

20. Alone. *By creating an environment similar to that of a flower growing on a vine, a dynamic spatial design is developed with the monkey chain as a strong vertical element. The white clematis is placed well off center so that it is possible for the eye to move beyond it; the flower is not trapped in the Japanese iron bucket but seems to float in space. Actual motion also occurs, for the basket sways with any stir of air. The dried wisteria creates many small diagonal spaces and forms one side of the large open triangle of the design. Japanese in feeling, individual in expression. Arranged by Lillian L. Bodine.*

21. Collage from Nature. *Garden forms, dried and pressed (except for the central cone "flowers"), include delicate grasses, the dramatic plume poppy (Bocconia cordata) at the top, Christmas ferns, broad croton leaves, and at lower left, a cluster of fine white cedar. The design is first set out on a wood panel framed with a brass binding. Then a sheet of white tissue is placed carefully above it and moistened to hold it. For permanence, a half-and-half solution of Elmer's Glue and water is plopped all over with a full soft brush, and this gives a lovely golden-beige tone to the collage. Finally, a hole is drilled for the pierced cone clusters. Notable for interesting contrast of shapes and textures and the well-considered open spaces within and around the design. Arranged by Lucy Sargent.*

22. Suspended in a Frame. *This free-hanging wall piece of weathered wood screwed to an open frame, fresh New Zealand flax leaves attached to the wood, and giant pink garlic blossoms represents a new interest of flower arrangers. The spaces in the design are as dominant as, if not more dominant than, the materials that create them—spaces between frame and outer shape, spaces made by the bent leaves, and the network of spaces within the wood. The garlic blooms further emphasize the two spaces they occupy and the openness of the design. A fine contemporary expression. Arranged by Bernice Kinney.*

23. Warp and Woof. *The longer we look at this assemblage, whose outline is defined by a frame, the more we discover in it. The dried natural forms of round lotus pods fastened on small dowels, the moving rhythm of the linear kelp, the accenting sprays of white nandina, and the green staghorn fern in a hanging ceramic vase are organized in a design whose elements are placed against a strong horizontal and vertical grid. This is developed by various weights and textures of black and turquoise yarn and string to divide the shallow space within the frame. The target lotus pods create the rhythm or time that moves through the space. A delightful picture for a contemporary setting. Arranged by Frances Bode.*

40

24. Conversation. *Suggesting a surrealistic discussion between two people—one tall and thin, one short and fat—a pair of green bottles hold pale dried kelp and starbursts of umbrella grass (cyperus). The design, full of humor and sparkle, animates the spatial area of the frame. Arranged by Frances Bode.*

25. Delicate Harmony. *In a pair of shells suspended by lengths of raffia, two pink roses reach vertically up, three reach horizontally out to develop a spatial tension that relates the two groupings and creates a central space as important as either of the shell-and-flower designs. Secondary spaces are found in the raffia enclosures. An expression of deceptive simplicity and romantic appeal. Arranged by Lee Early Quinn.*

42

26. For a Porch Wall. *A dark rough slab supports pink peonies and a bud, which move away from the wood to give a dynamic balance and develop a relationship of the whole to the wall. The iron scroll supports the dark basket, which holds a copious supply of water. A simple and effective decoration. Arranged by Marguerite Bozarth.*

27. Outdoor Decoration. *Pink bleeding-hearts, flowers rarely used in arrangements, are charmingly displayed in a rich brown bamboo basket hung against a smooth light-tan board, an appropriate background for such intricate material. The cluster of flowers and foliage above and the sparse pendent branch below outline an effective space, and asymmetric balance is skillfully achieved. Arranged by Marguerite Bozarth.*

44

Decorative Wood. *28. Above. A gray-and-yellow wall decoration with curves of pussy willow balanced against a curve formed by the daisies, acacia, and a fine wood structure. A natural opening at the top conceals moist Oasis that keeps the flowers fresh. The space created by the willow lines gives a lightness that visually supports the design in space. 29. Right. A tan-to-brown symphony is distinguished by a double triangle of wood with a pocket holding dried desert artichokes, glycerined magnolia leaves, and palm fronds with black seeds. Here a harp form is suggested with an open space, which is an important aspect of the composition. Arranged by Mary G. Knight.*

30. Contemporary Easter Basket. *A far cry from the traditional, this handmade container by Reba Harris, in a form suggesting an epergne with a series of open spaces at different levels, hangs on a yellow-painted door to welcome Easter guests. The basket, woven from natural strands of the queen palm, holds yellow and orange tulips and clusters of white azalea, these kept fresh in soaked Oasis covered with wire and fastened to the side of the basket so as not to obscure its pattern of open spaces in contrast to the opposing mass of flowers. Moss-green velvet ribbon sets off the harmony of flowers and background. Arranged by Marianna Brockway.*

31. For the Easter Luncheon. *This unique decoration of brown and white plastic eggs, green leatherleaf fern, and yellow and white marguerites (both well conditioned and kept fresh in concealed Oasis) is suspended by almost invisible monofilament from the dining-room chandelier above the center of the table. The suspended decoration leaves the whole table free for the buffet. Arranged by Marianna Brockway.*

32. Easter Decoration Upstairs. *A dainty eye-level bouquet hangs in the organdy-curtained window of the bedroom in colors that harmonize with the yellow-and-blue wallpaper there. A white half-basket suspended from a picture hook lies flat against the casement and supports the dried flowers and pressed fern in a Styrofoam block. Pale to deep yellow strawflowers, 'Coronation Gold' achillea, Canadian goldenrod (sprayed with a fixative to check fluffing), white and yellow statice, and white baby's-breath with touches of turquoise-blue painted skyrockets carry out the color scheme with bow and streamers of yellow velvet ribbon. Arranged by Marianna Brockway.*

33. For Any Season. *A simple basket of yellow carnations, set off by eucalyptus foliage, is almost invisibly suspended to make a winter party decoration. With these flowers available the year round, this design of good balance and open spatial outline that decorates without crowding could grace other seasons. Designed by Harry A. Lazier.*

50

34. For an Evening Wedding. *The lamppost by the bridge is lighted and decorated to guide wedding guests down the brook path. From the summer garden, white hydrangeas coming into full bloom, double shasta daisies, and tips of pachysandra are fashioned into a fresh Styrofoam-based nosegay design, the flowers kept fresh in water tubes, which give directional freedom, and set off by a white satin streamer. Arranged by Marianna Brockway.*

35. Door Decoration for a Summer Wedding. *A vertical white-rose, white-ribbon, and white-candle design welcomes guests and highlights the occasion. Flowers are supported and kept fresh in a plastic cup of moist Oasis, the whole wired to the candle sconce. (Photo 30 shows the same yellow front door with an Easter decoration.) Arranged by Marianna Brockway.*

36. For the Wedding Reception. *A decorated chandelier takes the place of a centerpiece, leaving the table free to set off the big wedding cake. Tight little bunches of white sweetheart roses and baby's-breath (flowers can be fresh, as here, and fastened in balls of Oasis, wires, and foil, or they may be dried or artificial). White ribbon bows and streamers are wired to the fixture; an unusual design to delight supper guests. Arranged by Marianna Brockway.*

54

37. Wedding Decoration. *Suspended in the hall, this gay design adds to the festive occasion. (It would also be appropriate for a porch party with echoing daisies in the garden.) A wicker birdcage, spray-painted antique green, provides an architectural structure, a central oblong with triangular spaces above and below. Tassels at top and bottom are unifying elements emphasized by flower placements, the tip daisy drawn through the upper triangle and turned toward the tassel but placed opposite to it. Below green-and-white myrtle tendrils curve in toward the lower tassel to integrate the design. The outline of flowers and vine makes many small outer spaces part of the design as a whole. Arranged by Mrs. Douglas P. Bryce.*

38. Harvest Swag. *Hung beside a pine mantel, this decoration is well suited to the season and to the colonial setting of paneling, pewter candlesticks, and black iron lantern. The swag includes the traditional corn—husks opened and turned up and down, also a multicolored ear—naturally dried brown and golden yarrow, and bright bunches of orange and yellow skyrockets. The velvet bow with long streamers sprayed soft brown completes an appropriate design of predominately earthy hues. Arranged by Marianna Brockway.*

56

39. Thanksgiving Dinner. *In her prerevolutionary house with pine wainscoting and mantel, Mrs. Brockway decorates her black tole "candelier" with bunches of green grapes, green apples, and English and Baltic ivy sprays threaded through the wires. (Soaked flat in water overnight, ivy keeps fresh for about twenty-four hours, longer if sprayed with fixative.) The green velvet bow is a nice finish for the high-up decoration, which is a delightful and convenient substitute for the conventional table centerpiece, the fruit decoration in keeping with Pilgrim tradition. Arranged by Marianna Brockway.*

40. For a Summer Wedding. *Suspended wire birds hold pink and red clusters of geraniums kept fresh in damp Oasis. While mobiles seldom include fresh materials, they are a possibility if properly handled. Arranged by Barbara S. Meisse.*

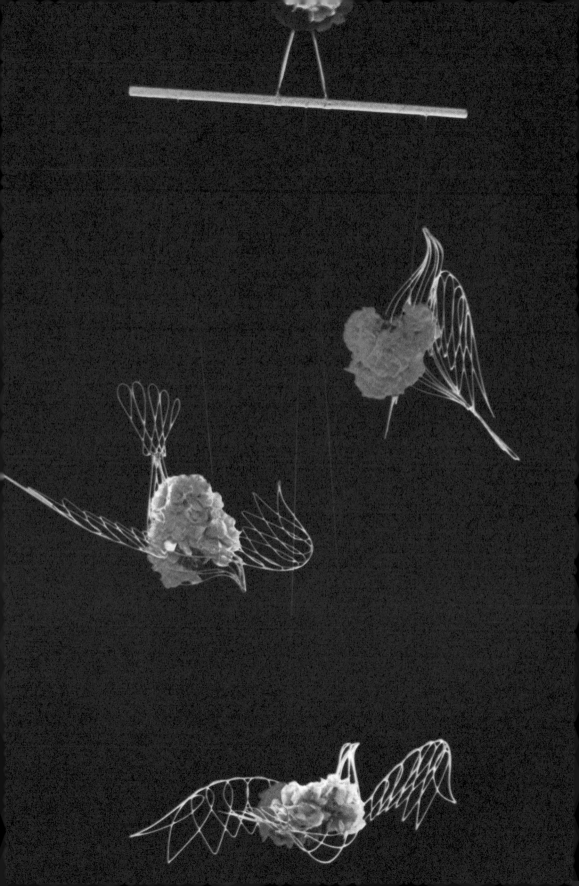

Thanksgiving in Williamsburg. *Handsome outdoor decorations in the colonial capital. These plaques are constructed on Styrofoam bases and hung by picture wire onto doors and railings to give the whole restored area a festive look. 41. Above. A platform railing is decorated with a center design of a pineapple for hospitality, red apples and yellow limes, and a circle of magnolia leaves; in the four corners are wise little echoes of the central motif. 42. Opposite top. Fastened to a paneled door is a similar design with cone roses and silver-edged ribbon. 43. Opposite bottom. This decoration for a slatted door is made with yellow lemons and green limes, brown pine cones, and magnolia leaves.*

44. Christmas Greeting in the Hall. *This new way with poinsettias—five chartreuse-white blooms with curled ti leaves and
dark tendrils of forced willow in a black iron lamp—displays
them above the heads of guests. Triangular forms occur through-
out—elongated in spaces outlined by the three chains, almost
equilateral in the mass of flowers with their pointed triangular
petals, also equilateral in the heavy lamp. The newer Mikklesen
and Eckes poinsettias last a long while if ends are cut, split, and
burned two inches up by match or candle flame, and the whites
and shades of pink are a pleasant change from red. Uncrowded
and lovely, this arrangement seems to float in space, like a
rhythm in the air. Arranged by Mrs. R. E. Agnew.*

45. Christmas Tree on High. *Gay with sparkle, a carved golden angel replacing the crystal drop at the base, this decoration employs the chandelier itself as a framework and follows its contours. Leatherleaf fern, conditioned to last almost indefinitely, forms the tree, which gleams, when lights are on, with tiny red and green balls and little bowknots of gold-sprinkled cord. (This is the same chandelier decorated high up for other seasons in photos 31 and 36.) Arranged by Marianna Brockway.*

46. Christmas Wreath. *To hang by a window or on a door, this modern wreath is actually a hoop covered with silver binding and decorated with shiny red ribbon bows and streamers. The green satin apples, clusters of gold ornaments, and star forms are set off by big green silk leaves. After its holiday exposure, this is stored, ready to decorate the house year after year—such a convenience. Arranged by Lois Wilson.*

64

47. Christmas in the Air. *Evergreen arbor vitae and brown hem-lock cones give a touch of nature to a design of hand-decorated Styrofoam balls that "freely spin a holiday greeting." Crossbars are cut from wire coat hangers, and balls hung by nylon fishline. Arranged by Mrs. James E. McGraw.*

66

II

They Float Through the Air
or Seem to–for Home or Show

> *Ingenious contrivances to facilitate motion,*
> *and unite levity with strength.*
>
> —Samuel Johnson

48. Orbital Dance, *1968*, DAVID BURT. *A mobile of brass flight shapes, washed in acid, hung in clusters, spinning on ball-bearing swivels—this is the epitome of motion, the changing forms exciting to watch. Collection of the artist.*

A present great enthusiasm of flower arrangers, and particularly of young moderns, is the mobile, suited to both home decoration and the flower show. High in the air, suspended from the ceiling, mobiles move freely, with symmetric or asymmetric balance, developing fascinating new patterns with every air-motivated turn. Stabiles are also fun to design. The stabile rests on table, floor, or ground but *looks* as if it were about to take off. However, its motion is implicit, not actual, and to me it is almost always comical. I do enjoy stabiles! The stamobile also has firm footing but one or more of its parts moves.

The mechanics of motion are not the province of this book, which is primarily concerned with design. To learn about knots and swivels, like those on fishing lines; proper suspension materials, as nylon monofilament; fine or heavy wire; heavy cotton (choice depends on the weight of the mobile elements); and the methods of organization, symmetrical or asymmetrical—all of which assure motion—consult one of the excellent books on the subject. (*How to Make Mobiles* by John Lynch, The Viking Press, 1968, gives clear explanations with step-by-step diagrams and photographs of completed mobiles.)

Some mobiles are balanced with parts that move or may move all at once; others, more complex, are designed so that motion originating in one area motivates motion in another. It is important that the parts of a mobile move readily in natural or forced air currents, that no part ever strikes against another, and that the design is pleasing from every point of view and every turning. You can make armatures from light or heavy wire, bent coat hangers, pieces of driftwood, or something else of your own choice; the purpose is, as far as possible, to conceal mechanics or to make mechanics part of the design. In any case, avoid the clunky look.

Alexander Calder, famous as the first designer of mobiles, also designed stabiles and stamobiles, though he did not use this last term.

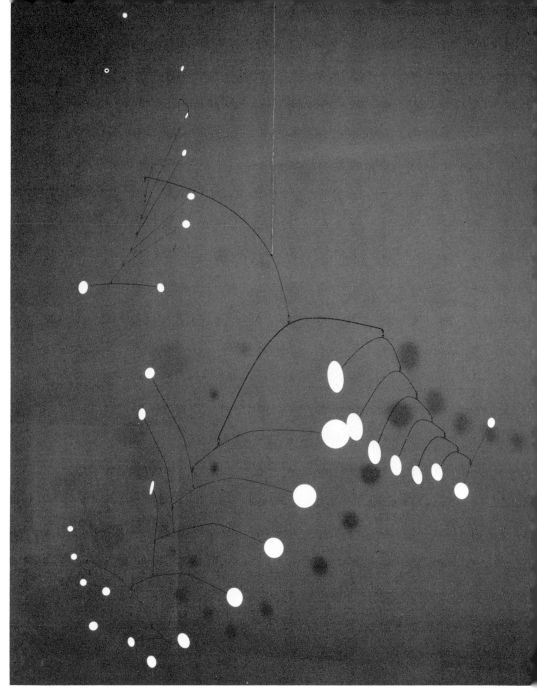

49. Snow Flurry, *1948*, ALEXANDER CALDER. *This tremendous hanging mobile, ninety-four by seventy inches, looks like a space drawing. Constructed of painted sheet metal and steel wire, in motion it gives a delightful illusion of snowflakes. Collection, The Museum of Modern Art, New York. Gift of the artist.*

(It was Esther Hamél who coined the word and described the type in *The Encyclopedia of Judging and Exhibiting,* Ponderosa, 1968.) In museums and galleries, you can study delightful variations of these three art forms not only by Calder but by Joseph Zalewski, George Rickey, and more recently David Burt, whose shaped and molded sculptural elements make his mobiles exciting and beautiful when new designs evolve in space, folding and extending as currents of air initiate motion.

Mobiles are constructed of metal, wood, glass, cardboard, paper, or plastic, and decorative designs for Christmas may even combine some of these (photo 47). The flower arranger usually prefers to create with dried grasses, reeds, leaves, blossoms, bark, even shells, or to include some natural elements with the non-floral. Mobiles with fresh flowers are difficult because these must be of a type that once well conditioned will last for a long time without water, or if dependent on it, can be kept fresh in some concealed water tubes or with Oasis (photo 40).

50. Birds. *Moved by gentle indoor currents, this mobile gives the effect of birds in flight. It is hung in a high-ceilinged living room against a window wall through which real birds are seen outside flying around a feeder. It is made entirely of natural materials. The top crossbar of this mobile is a weathered branch (rather than a metal rod), and the "birds" are sycamore bark peelings, oiled with linseed to prevent drying, and left in natural form with no special shaping. Arranged by Harriet Kenney.*

72

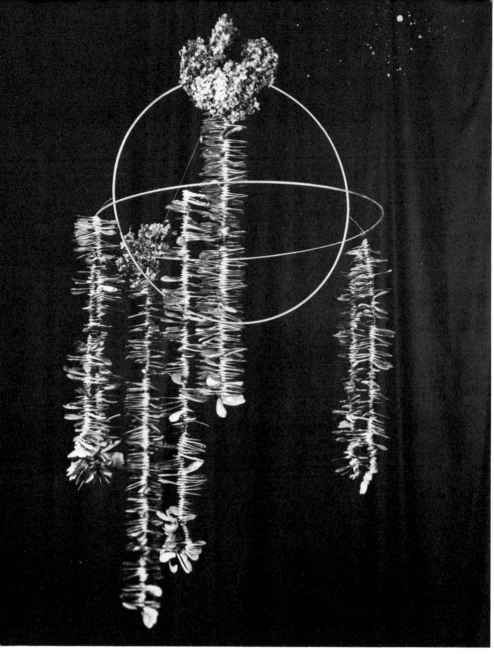

51. **Hoops and Hydrangeas.** *A mobile based on two brass hoops hung from nylon monofilament with a brass fishing swivel at the top is made of dried materials—two clusters of cinnamon-brown hydrangeas, one for each hoop, and five long strands of yellow maple "keys" or seed pods. Color and charm are enhanced by the flashes of brass as the hoops turn in air. Arranged by Barbara S. Meisse.*

52. **From Nature.** *Suspended from the edge of the porch roof of a summer cottage with the ocean for background, this mobile consists of two natural wood sections found within feet of each other on the beach. Smooth and pure white, the central piece suggests a seahorse for which the four-foot oval, also of bleached wood, makes a frame. Here is a mobile without special mechanics, of wood requiring no special treatment. Hung with a double thread from the balanced center of the arching piece (this suspended from a beam), the seahorse moves in the ocean breeze, presenting a fine design at every turn. Arranged by Harriet Kenney.*

53. **On the Prowl.** *This five-foot stabile is open to interpretation: perhaps a jolly animal dressed in an impossible garment and on the prowl, hesitating only long enough to have its picture taken. As with abstract designs generally, the more we look, the more we see. The design, original in conception, is rich in humor and with the imminent sense of motion essential to every stabile. Fan palm, contorted mullein, hydrangea, and driftwood provide strong contrasts of shapes and textures. Arranged by Nelda H. Brandenburger.*

54. Emergence, *1969,* DAVID BURT. *This great figure of welded copper and bronze on the beach might be called a stabile, so implicit is its motion. It stirs the imagination. Is it a giant sea animal just emerging from the depths, a great hawk, a Japanese Kabuki performer with draperied arms extended for the next movement of the dance? Collection of the artist.*

55. Assemblage with a Difference. *Here positive space is experienced in the openings of gears and curled lengths of rattan, and these are lively with motion. The allium heads are spray-painted orange; the skillful balance of foliage is loquat. Arranged by Nelda H. Brandenburger.*

56. Diagonal with Flowers. *A rusted metal discard is used as container, not accessory, for an in-the-air sculpture. Geometric areas were opened up with a hack saw and stature increased with a base, pedestal, and finial, the welding done by a professional. A diagonal of day lilies makes a forceful line with two furled aspidistra leaves for transition. In this statement, sculpture and flowers associate with distinction. Arranged by Marianna Brockway.*

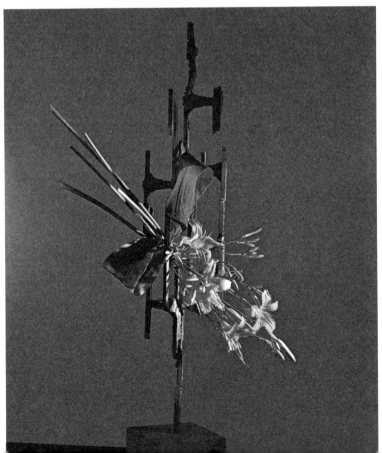

57. Mobile from Japan. *Edgeworthia* (*mitsumata*), *painted white and touched with pink, and graduated paper cones, also white and pink, make an unusual five-part mobile with balance achieved by different weights on long and short cords. Arranged by Kasumi Teshigahara, Vice President, Sogetsu School, Tokyo.*

58. Stabile with Space. *An assemblage in its assortment of found objects—a gooseneck lamp sprayed flat gray, a section of orange-brown sandblasted driftwood, and circles of starry green parsnips from the wild—this design is really a stabile. It rests on a table but appears ready to walk off. Motion is more than implicit here, and that fine central space formed by the double curves commands as much attention as any of the elements or the design as a whole. Stabiles amuse me. This design has the whimsical quality I find in most of them, and here a shadow appears to chase the fleeing object. Arranged by Mrs. Christopher Z. King.*

59. Assemblage-Stabile. *Motion is implied in this stabile design that stands on a table. Here a collection of metal pieces from a junkyard is welded into an assemblage that serves as support for purple allium heads and eucalyptus branches. The curved central shaft is balanced by the horizontal thrust of the plant materials, and the welded structure encloses space at the top and at the base. Arranged by Nelda H. Brandenburger.*

60. In Stride. *This stabile occupies more than the space. Indeed the design scarcely holds to the page as the driftwood limbs stride boldly off to some important appointment on the left. (Lady in a flowered hat hurrying to a board meeting?) Such action-compositions are fun to make and amusing to look at. The sense of motion usually depends on the shape of the base, here a fortuitous piece of self-supporting wood that initiates the upward thrust into space. Plant material is restricted to five garlic seed heads and a couple of kalanchoe leaves. Arranged by Marlie L. Erwin.*

61. Spider, *1939,* ALEXANDER CALDER. *This complex six-foot standing mobile or stabile of painted sheet aluminum and steel wire is suspended from a shape that stands on the floor instead of hanging from the ceiling. The linked clusters of small moving objects on the left are balanced by the movement of the large bobbing rudder form on the right. Here humor adds to our delight in the design. Collection, The Museum of Modern Art, New York. Gift of the artist.*

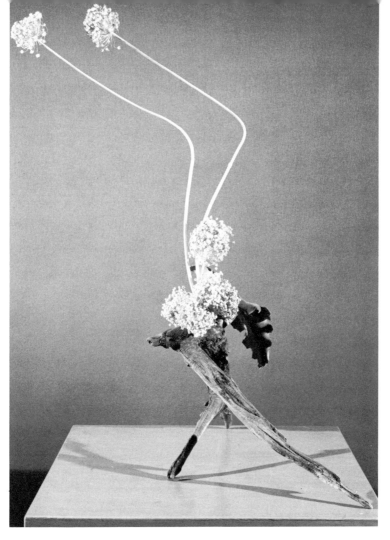

62. Christmas in Swingtime. *This stamobile, based upon a rhythmic wind-blown, black-sprayed branch—that alone is full of motion—is bright with starry forms suspended from the branches. These are made from inch-diameter Styrofoam balls, covered with black poster paint (not enamel or lacquer, which causes shriveling). Into each ball some fifty or more stems of tiny Mexican everlasting strawflowers have been inserted, one color to a star—red, orange, hot pink, blue, lavender, and green. In motion, this gives the effect of a kaleidoscope of brilliant color. Arranged by Muriel L. Merrell.*

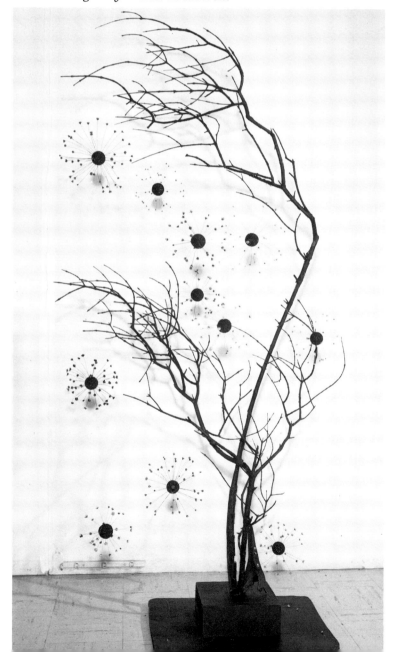

63. Circus Escape. *Originally staged for a judges' symposium, this driftwood stamobile, with a purposeful surrealistic air, was a vision of moving light and changing pattern. Set on a nineteen-inch-square stand, thirty inches high, and covered with a quarter-inch-thick lucite top, it was illuminated by a 150-watt spotlight placed under the color wheel. This was kept in motion by a little motor. The effect was most arresting when one color was moving off and a second one was mixing with it, the suspended parts (seen here at the left) gently changing their forms. Such motorized pieces have caught the imagination of designers who like to experiment with actual motion rather than simply suggesting it. Arranged by Frances Bode.*

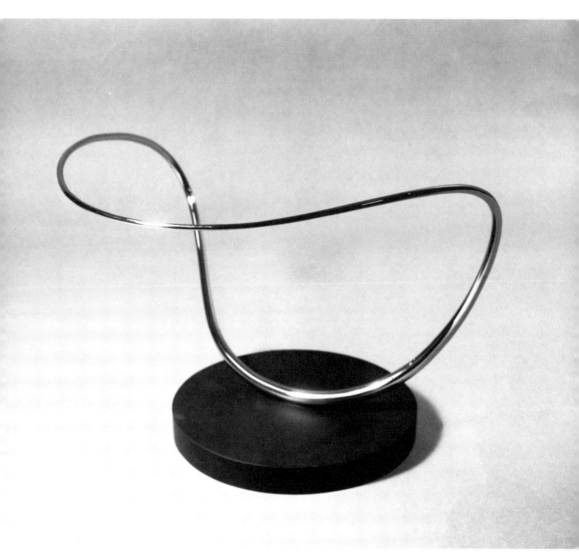

III

They Incorporate Space and Motion as Design Elements—for the Flower Show

> *The modern artist, by nature and destiny, is always an individualist.*
>
> —Herbert Read

64. Construction 8, 1954, JOSÉ DE RIVERA. *A forged rod of stainless steel produces a design of exquisite simplicity, moving in its beauty, and an inspiration to designers whose preference is for linear rather than mass compositions. The subtle bending of the line creates curved planes of space and a sense of volume. Collection, The Museum of Modern Art, New York. Gift of Mrs. Heinz Schultz in memory of her husband.*

As we consider the art of today, we may feel that it appeals more to our intellect than to our emotions, that there is more meaning and less beauty—in the traditional sense—to be found in contemporary work. It seems to require concentration for most of us to appreciate a modern artist's painting or sculpture. We compare our reaction to architecture. From Gothic we experience immediate exaltation; Renaissance palaces and churches require understanding. At art exhibits and flower shows we notice that only the knowledgeable seem to experience an immediate flush of pleasure, a sweep of joy. For most of us it takes time to divine the contemporary artist's purpose, to experience his statement. And each of us must find his own meaning.

It is easy to enjoy a colorful painting of purple and white lilacs, so vivid we can almost smell them, or a sculpture of a smiling child holding a turtle. It is something else to be exhilarated by Seymour Lipton's *Imprisoned Figure* or Mary Callery's *Symbol A.* Until we cease to apply the old criteria and open our minds to the new, modern art—and modern flower arrangements—are likely to be enigmas. But when we commence to search for meanings instead of resenting the unfamiliar, a new world of artistic excitement opens to us, for beauty is not of one kind, one style; and true to the cliché, it *is* in the eye of the beholder.

In 1957 Henry Moore, whose massive nudes are familiar in many museums, made this statement:

> *Vitality and power of expression.* For me a work must first have a vitality of its own. I do not mean a reflection of the vitality of life, of movement, physical action, frisking dancing figures and so on, but that a work can have in it a pent-up energy, an intense life of its own, independent of the object it may represent. When a work has this powerful vitality we do not connect the word Beauty with it.

Beauty, in the later Greek or Renaissance sense, is not the aim of my sculpture.

Between beauty of expression and power of expression there is a difference of function. The first aims at pleasing the senses, the second has a spiritual vitality which for me is more moving and goes deeper than the senses.

Because a work does not aim at reproducing natural appearances it is not, therefore, an escape from life—but may be a penetration into reality . . . an expression of the significance of life, a stimulation to greater effort in living.

It is this "penetration into reality" that serious flower arrangers seek to express in their work. Like Archipenko, they often use interior negative space as positive sculptural form, and they are fond of disparate and unorthodox materials. They no longer look on space as something to be filled, but rather as an element moving in, around, and outside a design to give it life. We experience this in Barbara Hepworth's *Curved Form with Inner Form* (photo 5) and in Moore's *The Bride* (photo 6). In the latter our response is purposely slowed by wire barriers drawn across space, and by this means depth is more vividly experienced.

Perhaps the keenest influence on arrangers today is that of the Constructivists, although Naum Gabo and Antoine Pevsner gave the main emphasis to the idea as early as 1922, and, as Sir Herbert Read states in *A Concise History of Modern Sculpture,* "a will to abstraction became manifest more or less simultaneously in several countries." In 1925 Gabo declared that "Art formerly reproductive has become creative," and the pieces he and his brother exhibited in Paris in 1924 included new materials like glass and plastic to express a new sense of space and dynamic rhythm. The aim of Constructivists like Gabo was to create structures that are a vital image of space and time. As Gabo himself wrote: "In a constructive sculpture, space is not a part of the universal space surrounding the object; it is a material by itself, a structural part of the object—so much so that it has the faculty of conveying a column as does any other rigid material."

Hilton Kramer once commented in *The New York Times:* "This notion of conceiving space itself as a form of sculptural mass was an idea of revolutionary import. It liberated sculpture from the use of monolithic materials such as stone and wood, permitting the sculptor to create forms that contained space and therefore light instead of displacing it." The floral designer has also been liberated to employ other than natural materials for structures that can hardly be termed flower arrangements, and through experimenting with a wide range of materials, knowledge of pure design has been increased.

Abstract design is a particular challenge. Plants are employed as pure geometric form—round, triangular, linear: a chrysanthemum is a round, yellow, abstract shape; a lily, a white triangle; stripped wisteria, a line; none of them, plants. Material is inverted, spray-painted, altered by trimming to suit a design, to develop a force. Flowers may be used without moisture since it has been discovered that certain ones, properly conditioned usually with chemicals in the water, stay fresh for the required span of a show. At flower shows many entries are placed high up at fifty inches or more above the floor. Pedestals are popular and often essential, for elevated designs are more plainly seen and give the best perspective for both spectators and judges.

Creativity and distinction—these are the qualities sought today. As Robert Motherwell puts it, "Each person sees a different picture depending on his culture." The flower arranger like every other artist seeks to relate, to communicate, to produce a truly personal expression. While scrupulously fulfilling the set demands of a class, each exhibitor lets imagination rather than "rules" dictate design. As a result, a refreshing originality characterizes the contemporary flower show. Few classes are now included for period pieces, and, while good traditional arrangement is pleasing, it is to the contemporary classes

65. Twinned Column, *1947,* ANTOINE PEVSNER. *In the 1930s, volume, physical mass, as earlier sculptors employed it, was rejected by this sculptor and his brother Naum Gabo, who sought to create with metals like this in bronze or with transparent plastics structures that were, as the brothers declared, "a vital image of space and time . . . real time." These two were among the first to use the contemporary materials of industry in sculpture; the result was a clean, machinelike sophisticated effect. Today the floral designer's interest in kinetic rhythm with a minimum of plant material, and that used strictly as form, has apparently developed from the ideas of the Constructivists. Courtesy, The Solomon R. Guggenheim Museum, New York.*

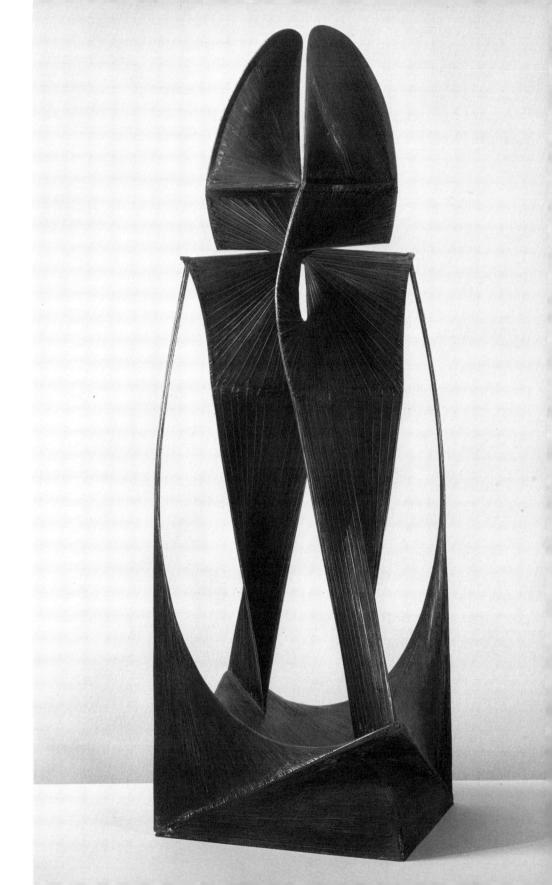

that the crowds flock, sometimes with bafflement, always with interest. And it is these classes that reflect the trends in other arts, particularly sculpture, which, as Read remarks, "has been the main agent of stylistic diffusion in modern times." Like the modern sculptor, the modern floral designer is working with electrically powered revolving tables on which designs and colors change with the slow revolutions.

In the exhibition pieces in this section, space or motion or both are emphasized as essential design elements. Environmental studies, also following the lead of sculpture designed for outdoors, represent a new range of interest. As Umberto Boccioni, the apostle of motion in sculpture, remarked, "We break open the figure and enclose it in environment."

66. Imprisoned Figure, *1948,* SEYMOUR LIPTON. *A seven-foot, wood-and-sheet-lead figure, which at the time may have had political significance, remains today as a fine example of Constructivist sculpture with the interior design seen through an exterior framework. Lipton and other sculptors of this period employed the convention of a frame of space, animated by internal forms and movements. It is interesting to compare this angularity and machinelike precision with the romantic quality of Hepworth's sculpture (photo 5). Collection, The Museum of Modern Art, New York. Gift of the artist.*

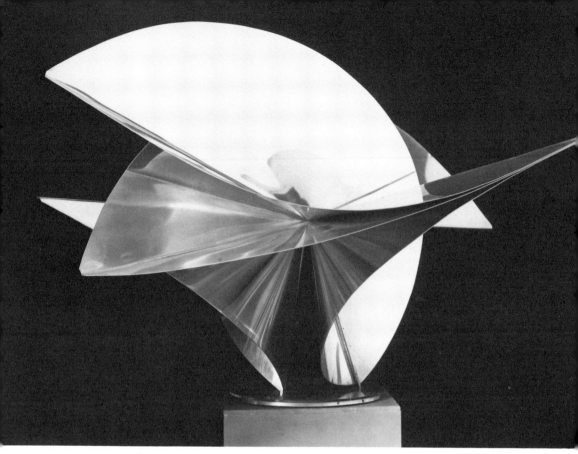

67. **Structure 14c**, *1961,* STEPHEN GILBERT. *This aluminum structure, a far cry from carved or modeled sculpture, speaks to us today. The interlocking planes are exciting in their space penetration, depth is realized from every point of view, and lightness suggests existence in space without the restraint of a pedestal. Courtesy, The Tate Gallery, London.*

68. Thrust into Space. *Inspired by Stephen Gilbert's sculpture in London's Tate Gallery, Mrs. Brockway makes an abstracted design with plant material to accompany her own aluminum structure. This is sprayed for black-to-white highlights and dimension, fastened to a black dowel, and inserted in a heavy wood block to support the high design in space, elongated by two tall gladiolus leaves. Two diagonals cross the perpendicular— one of shaped leaves, the other of the clear-stemmed, suspended flower stalk. (Well conditioned, the gladiolus requires no water. Also trustworthy without water are anthuriums, callas and other lilies, carnations, chrysanthemums, daylilies, iris, and strelitzias.) Repeated triangular spaces, within and without, characterize the exaggerated style of this contemporary design. Arranged by Marianna Brockway.*

94

69. Universe. *In the spirit of contemporary sculpture—abstract forms enclosing and creating space—this composition is constructed of joined sections of wood, metallic-finished (a laquer thinner rubbed through several coats of paint produced the effect), and brass wires inserted in the wood and across the openings to achieve a sense of depth. The fresh roses, fragile and ephemeral, are in contrast to the heavy wood—a strong statement. Arranged by Nelda H. Brandenburger.*

70. Rhythm. *Curves of palmetto sheath moving around a vertical of iris leaves create a rhythm that the eye follows from tip through central looping to the sharp, divided lower thrusts. A weathered wood sculpture, with a pocket drilled for a pinholder, provides steadying central emphasis and positioning for the yellow spuria iris and green leaves. This is an original design of spaces and graceful cadences. Arranged by Marianna Brockway.*

71. Spring. *Stylized, this offers a refreshing experience after so many years of spring, traditional. The airy statement held in space employs swirling diagonal loops of golden forsythia, forced and bent with gentle pressure, and a high-up central cluster of yellow daffodils and green leaves. A cedar stump with wood dowel holds a frog, a harbinger of spring, and elevates the nicely curved section of wood that conceals tubes and a cup of water for the fresh material. Arranged by Marianna Brockway.*

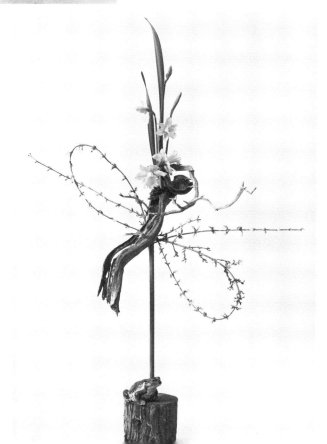

72. Seascape Collage. *Cleverly composed on a background of an enlarged photograph of a sailing vessel from an old encyclopedia, mounted on old wooden planks, this design includes a handsome crab from the Carnegie Museum that dominates the design, and seaweed and shells. The design has the shallow two-dimensional space of sculptural bas-relief. Designed by Lawrence Taylor.* Courtesy, The Orange Disc, *Gulf Oil Corporation.*

73. Loops of Space. *Inspired by Moore's "inside-inside" sculptures, Mrs. Bode prepared a framing of willow to rise from a brown ceramic. (The stripped branches, bundled and wrapped in copper wire, are baked in a low oven for an hour to make an amber hue, cooled, and painted with a half-and-half solution of Elmer's Glue and water to hold shape and give a sheen.) The willow makes four ovals within which are placed two round agapanthus seed heads and two reddish philodendron leaves of triangular shape—the result, a dramatic and formal design with strong spatial interest. Arranged by Frances Bode.*

74. Cage of Space. *Like Lipton's* Imprisoned Figure *(photo 66), this study in motion has inner as well as outer form within a cage. In the volume created by the branches, two leaves establish a secondary inner movement, slow on the right, down, rising quickly on the left. In contrast, the massive central form of aeonium revolves on a different axis in a slower, circular, but off-center path. Equilibrium is maintained by the heavy usubata pedestal. Arranged by Bernice Kinney.*

75. Shelter. *This expressive free form, bold and dramatic, catches us up in its whirling sweep. Movement is initiated by the roundness of the ceramic, which itself seems in motion as it draws the eye toward the spiral cut of the brim, and from there up through curves of foliage and flowers to the lines of bleached broom. These delineate a small, safe inner world of space, with depth, in which the tulips are enclosed, and it is this space, working in counterpoint to the spiraling movement, that helps create the harmony of the whole. The strong base anchors the active design, which suggests the form-within-form sculptures of Moore and Lipton. Arranged by Stella Coe.*

Studies in Crossed Lines. *Space and motion are well expressed by these two Japanese free-style arrangements, both with clean sparse lines of crossing arcs in space. 76. Right top. The black-painted desert primrose introduces a texture repeated at the base by the cluster of cut lengths of grass, all in good balance above the horizontal tray. 77. Right bottom. Swamp willow emerges from two openings in a vase which is also modeled in a crossed design, its lines continued by the exuberant willow. The opening in the container relates in feeling to the white chrysanthemums, both acting as anchors. Arranged by Lee Early Quinn.*

102

78. Verticality. *This tall construction consists of three vertical shapes, two of wood and one of space. The floating boundary of space on the far right is counterbalanced by rubber-plant leaves and a seed-pod flower form, a group which gives an interesting outline to the space on the far left. This work achieves the monumentality that is an intrinsic quality of good sculpture. Arranged by Mrs. Merritt England.*

79. Time in Space. *Symbolic of our age, this composition has a weightless quality achieved through the balance and relationship of the abstract sculptural forms—designed and made by Mrs. Fisher—and the plant material preserved by her. The kelp defines the vertical space and serves as transition through the separate parts of the design. A dynamic expression of motion in space as "new" today as when it received the Fenwick Medal in 1963. Arranged by Mrs. Roswell E. Fisher.*

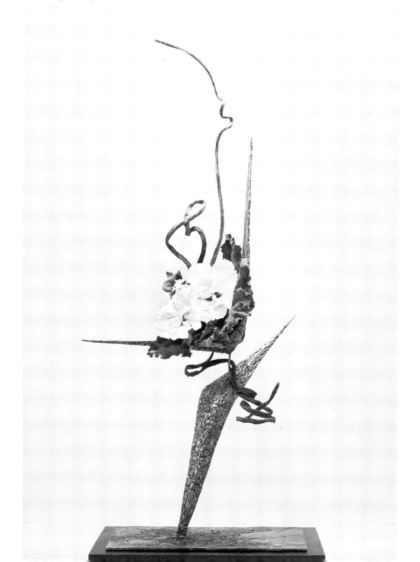

80. Reclining Figure, *1938,* HENRY MOORE. *Even small pieces by this sculptor—this one measures only about six by thirteen inches—have the quality of monumentality. The figure is abstracted, and the spaces which we look into and through assume as much weight and importance as the solids of the composition. Collection, The Museum of Modern Art, New York.*

81. Vital Spaces. *In this composition two spaces are enclosed by
the tortuous lines of roots. The eye would be held to these spaces
were it not for the measured placement of celosias and aspidistra leaves, which in turn establish other balancing spaces. The
grapes act as accent and transition from inner to outer spaces.
Arranged by Mrs. Merritt England.*

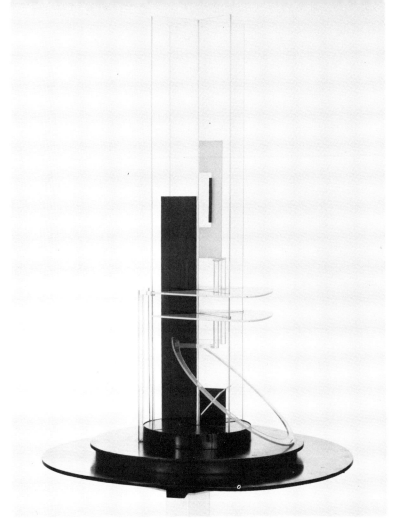

82. Column, *1923*, NAUM GABO. *Plastic, wood, and metal are used in a construction of far-reaching effect. Today, plastics, sometimes combined with colored lights and motion, are increasingly popular with contemporary sculptors. In their 1920 Constructivist Manifesto, Gabo and Pevsner abandoned "volume . . . and mass as structural elements" and maintained that "depth [is] the one form of space." Courtesy, The Solomon R. Guggenheim Museum, New York.*

83. Plastic Power. *Like the Constructivists, the flower arranger employs new materials to convey a sense of depth, space, and dynamic rhythm. In this design, swirling plastic rods defining spatial areas appear to be set in motion by the glass discs that serve as raised bases for horizontal and vertical boxes. These are made of plastic strips through which are seen the white orchids. Both form and material suggest Gabo's Column (above). Rhythmic and delicately beautiful. Arranged by Mary E. Thompson.*

108

84. Composition 19—Symbol A, *1960,* MARY CALLERY. *A steel and brass space drawing makes a powerful statement with spatial planes and flowing lines, as in cursive writing. When the eye follows the dynamic rhythms of this design, space becomes tangible. Courtesy, M. Knoedler & Co., Inc., New York.*

85. Contrasts. *In an elevated black-and-orange ceramic, a firm structure of nailed driftwood pieces, stained brown, is accented by rounded forms of tangerine carnations with a soft transition of feathery nandina foliage. The lines and spaces of the wood are repeated in reverse in the decoration of the container; the linear pattern suggests Mary Callery's* Symbol A *(above). Arranged by Nelda H. Brandenburger.*

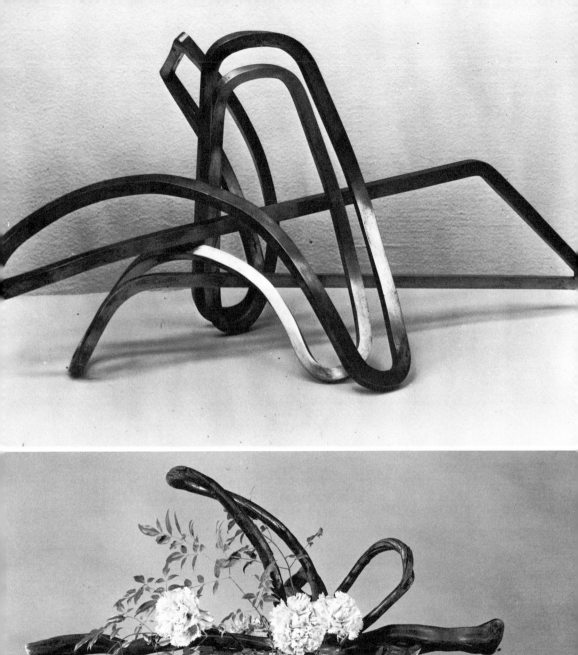

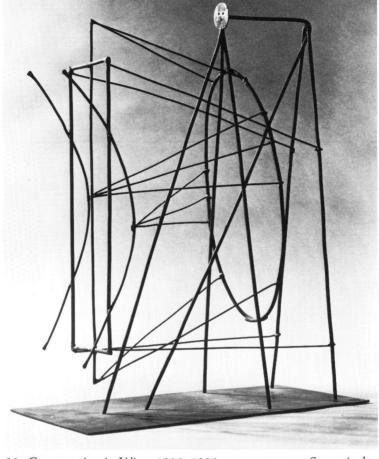

86. Construction in Wire, *1928–1929*, PABLO PICASSO. *Space is defined here by wire outlines—a drawing in space, quite different from the traditional solidity of sculpture or the early mass designs of flower arrangement. Linear designs today relate to this earlier structure composed of pure line and space. Mobiles also evolved from such space cages, adding movement to create ever-changing spatial relationships. Permission SPADEM, 1970, by French Reproduction Rights, Inc. Collection of the artist.*

87. Geometric Abstract. *Vanishing-point perspective lines drawn in black India ink on an orange background develop spatial relationships for three pink anthuriums, two of whose black-painted vertical stems reinforce the geometry. In contrast to the linear precision, a subdued counterpoint is afforded by the curves of flower forms, the wired third stem, the rounded openings and supports of the ceramic, and the ovoid polished base. Emphasis is on the construction and on clean, well-defined space, the intervals as interesting as the solids. Space beneath the container is also important. The design suggests Picasso's* Construction in Wire *(above). Arranged by Mrs. William Burger.*

88. Windswept. *Dynamic counterbalance is achieved in this por-*
trayal of gale-force wind without a single prop. The material—
pale bleached broom with spaces between the groupings, and
one dark arum leaf—speaks for itself. We sense depth as the
delicate white lines of broom placed over the leaf let us see
through to darker areas below, and this horizontal leaf relates
to the wild movement of the design. Through the overlay of
broom, the leaf is prevented from becoming a deadening hori-
zontal while contributing anchorage to the container, and this
also has a part in motivating the linear movement of the design
in space. Off-balance composition can be seen in many contem-
porary sculptures, as in Robert Bart's Untitled, 1964 *(opposite).*
Arranged by Stella Coe.

114

89. Untitled, *1964*, ROBERT BART. *More than five feet tall, this aluminum sculpture challenges the equilibrium and arrests motion in a stimulating off-balance design. Collection, The Museum of Modern Art, New York. Gift of Philip Johnson.*

90. Precarious Balance. *In this semiabstract, the containing device—a car spring welded at an acute angle to a tripod stand—creates a problem in balance that is solved in a lofty design of driftwood, monstera foliage, and dahlias. Where imbalance is so pronounced, the viewer is forced to take an active part in establishing equilibrium, and herein lies the vitality of this work. The three major spaces in the composition have different perceptional qualities. Strongest is the compressed space, lower left, which seems physically to keep the design from falling; next in strength is the long space described by the branches and enriched by serrated leaves; the third, more passive, space is to the right. Spatial compression can also be seen in Robert Bart's* Untitled, 1964 *(preceding page). Arranged by Mary E. Thompson.*

116

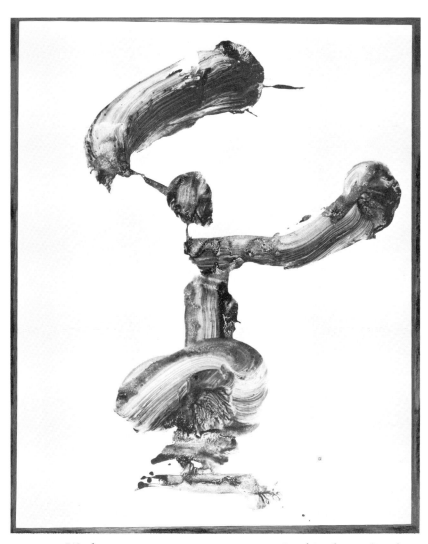

91. Work 63-14-3, *1963*, NANKOKU HIDAI. *In this almost five-foot brush-and-ink painting, we can feel the action of the artist's arm as he moves the brush over the surface of the paper. The rhythmic motion and the space that it describes are the life of the work, and space here is sculptural. The bold design suggests many forms found in nature. Collection, The Museum of Modern Art, New York. Gift of Dr. Frederick Baekeland.*

92. **Wood Form.** *Constructed of weighty sections of wood doweled together and heavily sprayed black to a velvety sheen, this three-foot abstract that looks rather like a black iron sculpture stands on a table in a garden with a redwood fence background. The round opening suggests the pierced sculpture of Hepworth and Moore; the heavy textured line, the Hidai brush-and-ink study (photo 91). A fine environmental ornament to enjoy out-of-doors. Arranged by Mrs. Merritt England.*

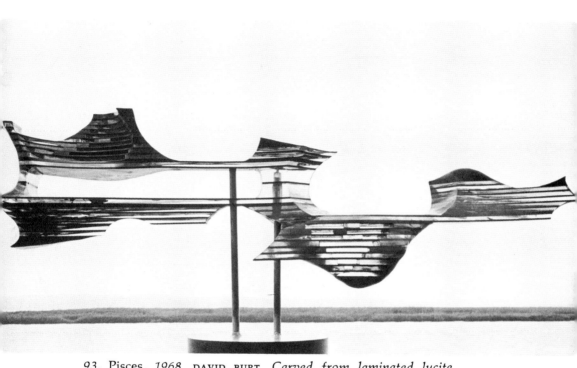

93. Pisces, *1968,* DAVID BURT. *Carved from laminated lucite, rather than developed by the hammered metal technique of earlier sculptures, this handsome maritime figure is a stimulating prototype for those planning environmental designs. Collection of the artist.*

94. In a Brook. *New to the flower artist's world is the environmental piece placed in an outdoor setting and changed with the seasons or the decorative purpose, as for a garden party. This handsome construction, set directly in my sunny brook, is mounted on heavy dowels in a wooden base. (For a permanent outdoor setting, the armature is made of weatherproof metals, aluminum or iron covered with rustproof paint, or left to rust naturally.) This design, suggested by David Burt's Pisces, consists of edgeworthia, streaked black and white; bleached palm; and a seven-foot column of cattails inserted in a heavy pinholder and placed in the bed of the brook. The rock seen behind the construction is an important focal form that increases depth perception. Arranged by Marianna Brockway.*

95. On the Beach. *Originally designed for a flower show, this interpretive piece is rich in symbolism, "the elements chosen to represent an eclipse of the sun by the earth as seen from Apollo 12." But like any successful design, it stands on its own merit and can be enjoyed by a viewer free to find his own meaning or interpretation. In the exhibition hall, the fantasy was heightened by the glow of ceiling spotlight and blinker, the light playing on the structure and the surface of the lilies giving the effect of motion. On the beach in natural light, we are also conscious of implied circular motion and aware of exciting spatial areas and balances. The two settings illustrate contemporary trends, special lighting and outdoor placements. Arranged by Marianna Brockway.*

96. Bird Forms. *A beautiful sight on a rocky Connecticut beach where the black-painted palmettos suggest dark bird forms, this study was originally designed for a show in an art gallery. There, as the structure revolved on a concealed one-rpm turntable (one revolution per minute), the reflexed "wings," molded in-the-round, cast deep shadows, and shapes changed within the design and also without, for this was essentially a "space-modifier." Here in an outdoor environment the structure is stationary, but motion is strongly implied, for the design seems to revolve as we view it. Arranged by Marianna Brockway.*

122

97. Water and Wood. *An exciting environmental sculpture appears in an equally exciting environment in California—in a pool with a waterfall behind it. Handsome in the setting, the six-foot structure of Sierra-found striated wood is made in two doweled sections for easy transport: the "flowers" contrived from araucaria pods with centers of Styrofoam, the foliage glycerined loquat, all the material realistic, long-lasting, and waterproof. While environment more or less affects all art, in this situation the movement and sound of water in contrast to the stable architectural structure is particularly effective. (Environmental pieces are not without hazard, half of this structure having been rescued from the flood by the intrepid photographer.) Arranged by Frances Bode.*

Helpful Reading

Goldwater, Robert, *What Is Modern Sculpture?* New York, The Museum of Modern Art, 1969.

Lynch, John, *How to Make Mobiles.* New York, The Viking Press, 1968.

Read, Herbert, *A Concise History of Modern Sculpture.* New York, Frederick A. Praeger, 1964.

Photo Credits

Index

About the Author

Helen Van Pelt Wilson—the author of more than a dozen books on flower arrangement (including twenty years of the first *Flower Arrangement Calendar*), on home gardening, and on house plants, contributor to national magazines, and an internationally known editor and speaker—has recently been fascinated by the very new look of floral designing in both home decoration and show work. Visits to the museums and galleries of Europe, Canada, and the United States have impressed her with the influences of the other arts on flower arrangement, and she explores these influences in this book.

Mrs. Wilson is a member of many horticultural societies and a fellow of the Royal Horticultural Society; she is included in *Who's Who of American Women* and *Foremost Women in Communications*.